# #Relationship Hacks

*7 Tips to Help Single Women Avoid Unhealthy Relationships*

**By**

**Quantia Isom**

Published by iCHAMPION Publishing

P.O. Box 2352 Frisco, TX 75034

Content edit by Nikia Hammonds-Blakely and iCHAMPION Publishing

Library of Congress Cataloging-in-Publication Data Publisher and Printing by iCHAMPION Publishing

Written By: Quantia Isom

Cover Design By: iCHAMPION Publishing

**ISBN: 978-1-7367112-3-1**

Self-Help

Personal Development

# Acknowledgements

First and foremost, I give the utmost to the Most High for allowing me to take a thought and manifest it into a book. For affording me the opportunity to meet a wonderful publicist that would help me share my story with others. Father, you never cease to amaze me! Won't He do it!

I am thankful for my sons, Marquez, Da'Von, Shimar, Malachi and granddaughters, Karter and Simara. They are my heartbeats and have always been the motivation behind my accomplishments. This one is for you kids!!

Thank you, daddy, Virgil Isom, for all your wisdom, guidance, and unconditional love. Your passion and love for writing caused me to take interest in writing. I pray your book will be published soon.

Shout out to my little big sister Quantisha for encouraging me and reading my rough drafts, after a hard day of work and taking care of my nephews. Sis gave me some great ideas! She and I have endured some of the same hardships but still we rise!

A huge thank you to my prayer team that meets faithfully every week. Benita, Laisha and Tachelle. These prayer warriors prayed me through at least 2 chapters a week!

Thank you, Benita, for being a big sister in Christ. A solid and stable woman of God. An alpha female that kept me on my p's and q's. Always challenging me and pushing me to think higher, be and do better. You encouraged me to write the book and do it afraid, when I was shaking in my boots. You are the definition of a virtuous woman.

Shavonne, you are an amazing woman! Thank you for believing in me and being supportive in all of my endeavors.

Shamar and Pia, thank you ladies for your support, wisdom, and knowledge you shared with me to help create content for the book. Y'all are the best!

Thank you, Gladys Lewis, for encouraging me to share my story. If it hadn't been for your invitation to your daughter's book signing event, this idea would still be a thought.

Thank you to all the ones that abandoned me, ghosted me, rejected me, used, and abused me. God favors me and what you meant for bad, He used it for my good and His glory!

Thank you Nikia for cheering me on and praying me through until the end. I appreciate you and the iChampion Team for all your hard work and assisting me with bringing this vision into fruition.

There are many others I didn't mention. I would need several more pages. I appreciate all of you for your prayers, patience, and pouring nothing but love into me.

And to all of you ladies that will read this user-friendly book, you were the reason I invested time, money, and energy into this resource. You deserve to be treated like the Queen you are without subtracting from who you are. Blessings!

# CONTENTS

# Foreword

---∞·∞---

In the book of Genesis, God asks Noah to gather livestock in pairs and Noah did as requested. God knew that in this journey called life that two are definitely better than one. However, it's during that time of singleness that God is able to cultivate, add and subtract but also create an extraordinary individual.

When the time comes, He sends you a partner, or in this case the author Quantia Isom. She and I have shared countless stories, motivation and testimonies. We both have overcome and still battle issues related to romantic relationships. There is no better person I trust more to share my deepest hurts with besides God. This book will begin to reveal some nuggets that we have shared, disclose some tools to break the cycles, and illuminate women's greatest gifts. I was honored when my sister in Christ asked me to bless this book.

As the reader, your spirit will be truly blessed. So, get your highlighter ready, and even some tissues because I declare shackles are about to be broken! Strongholds removed and the glory of God is about to shine brighter. May God's will be done, In Jesus Name Amen.

Tachelle Price

# Introduction

———— ∞ ————

Relationships are similar to fashion. They will never go out of style unlike certain clothing items. Sorry, but polyester pants will never be part of my wardrobe. Relationships are always trending; have become the center of attention thanks to social media; and the main topic of everyday conversations.

Who has one? How did they get that one? Where did they get one? Can I get one like Ciara and Russel Wilson? I'm sure some of you have asked, what prayer did Ciara pray to get blessed with him? How did she catch him? Will it last? Are they a match made in Heaven? This couple is practically every woman's #relationship goal.

What about platonic friendships? Some of us desire a relationship like Gayle and Oprah. Two highly successful women that have an unbreakable bond like David and Jonathan in the Bible. They have weathered the storms together, empowered and encouraged each other to strive to new heights in their careers without being jealous and envious of one another.

Some of us just desire healthy relationships, period. Whether it's with the same sex, opposite sex, our mother and father, sister or brother. We are tired of investing in one-sided relationships. Giving more than we are getting. Being treated like options instead of a priority.

I have encountered numerous relationships over the years and have been subjected to rejection, abandonment, and abuse in various ways. Some of the hats I wear and have worn, in relationships are favorable and unfavorable. Mother, daughter, sister, friend, aunt, unfavored child, rebound, rebounder, side chick, mistress; you get the picture. Some of the relationships, as you guessed by the titles were obviously dysfunctional, unhealthy, and downright toxic.

I can recall having one of my greatest relationship epiphanies, while on a date, as we were discussing our exes. I was sharing my war stories. Looking like the victim. Pointing the finger at the men that had treated my heart like a football. How they tossed it 'to and fro', dropped it, and even kicked it at times. I was actually the one that passed it to them but it was their fault for mishandling it, right? I called "flag on the play".

He wasn't having it and sarcastically asked me, "who is the common denominator in all your failed relationships?" Oh no! It was me! Three fingers were pointing back at me! It looked like another "Love TKO" was on the horizon. I knew it was time to have a come to Jesus meeting with myself!

I went straight to the Creator and Designer of relationships, God Himself with all my relationship woes. I knew He had the solution(s) to the problem and could give me the answer(s) I needed to be victorious in this area. I knew He could fix whatever was broken, including me. I mean you wouldn't take your car to a construction worker to repair. You take it to the dealership or someone experienced in fixing cars. And even though God is the Creator of human beings and the Author of relationships, we exclude Him from our current and prospective relationships. We don't seek His approval or advice. How is that working for you?

Quite a few of us have adopted culture's way of obtaining and maintaining relationships instead of God's way. There might be some similarities but the wisdom of God will never mislead nor misguide you and will lead you to productive and prosperous relationships. My relationships are a lot healthier and fulfilling since I began seeking God. I discuss every potential and current relationship with Him.

Now I know there are tons of books, blogs, and vlogs, etc. on the subject of relationships but none told from my experiences, research, and perspective. Most of us have, or should have relationship goals and for us who do, we tend to look to parent's, celebrities, close friends, and other resources to help curate and customize our own. As I previously mentioned, first and foremost, I decided to look to God. His Word and other resources to generate tips that you can add to your relationship arsenal.

Keep in mind, one size doesn't fit all but, as you see on some clothing tags, one size fits most. There are 7 practical tips that can be applied to any relationship but mainly romantic ones. I pray the tips will help you get to the root cause of your failed and unfruitful relationships, uproot the problems or issues that are hindering you from fruitful and fulfilled relationships, and obtain breakthrough and victory, both now and in the future.

A short disclaimer, the stories I share are told from my vantage point and recollection of the encounters. The names of the parties are fictitious to protect the identity of the real culprits, I mean citizens of the United States. In all sincerity, I believe some of them are good people but not a good fit for me and others just need to be on the America's most wanted list to protect other people from their debauchery. In reality, they are broken individuals and need Jesus to make them whole. I don't hold any grudges and appreciate the lessons I learned from them. I allowed all of them to make me better and not bitter.

I added humor to keep you engaged but these experiences were real, painful, and far from funny when they occurred. I'm only sharing tidbits and a high-level overview of what I really endured. You have permission to laugh but I hope you are able to glean wisdom from my foolery at the same time.

# TIP # 1

# Don't Ignore The Red Flags

———◇·◇———

*"The same red flags you ignored in the beginning, will be the same reason it all ends"*

**– Unknown**

Red flags are like warning signs and signals alerting us that something is wrong.

> Red flags are like warning signs.

They can be subtle and easily missed. On the flipside, they can be very obvious like the check engine light on the dashboard of your car or the sign on the road that says "Danger, Do not Enter".Either way, they are trying to get your attention and make you aware of an issue and you shouldn't ignore it. But if you are like me, you sometimes see the red flags and pretend you are color blind. Or you notice the danger sign on the road and drive through anyways like you're immortal. For example, a man you are dating tells you he loves you after only knowing you for one week. This is called love bombing which is an early sign of manipulation and a red flag often missed. Men know what women want to hear and use it to their advantage.

Proverbs 22:3 says, "a prudent person foresees danger and takes precautions. But the simpleton goes blindly on and suffers the consequences." What a hefty price to pay when you don't take heed to the warnings.

I agreed with the comedian, Sommore, when she said men should come with warning labels. "Warning, will cause your hair to fall out, dance on your last nerve, cheat on shatter your heart into millions of pieces and flee to the next victim!" With all that being said, let me introduce you to whom I would like to call "Zaddy". My first love. You will know why this name fits him perfectly, momentarily.

I remember meeting the love of my life in my early 20's. Turns out, I wasn't the only love in his life. Zaddy had a different woman for everyday of the week, I later discovered. This man was quite older, more experienced and had my nose wide open! Zaddy had won me over with his good looks, smooth talk, and boyish charm. Skin the color and texture of Hershey's milk chocolate and a head crowned with dark wavy hair. He wasn't too tall or too short and possessed a natural muscular physique. Zaddy was just right! God's handiwork had been manifested in human flesh! He had impeccable taste when it came to clothes and always drove a flashy car.

Zaddy knew how to make you feel like you were the only woman in the world. I felt like the luckiest girl on the planet to be in his presence. He was different than the guys my own age because he actually understood me. Zaddy knew how to stimulate my mind and body. We had lots of mature conversations that ranged from religion, business, and goals. He was my Mr. Mcdreamy, so I thought. However, Zaddy was deceptive from the beginning but I was too young and naive to recognize the red flags. I definitely paid the price with my heart, esteem, and many other consequences because I missed the warning signs. He turned out to be Mr. Mcnightmare!

Let me give you some background on how we met. I had started seeing him around town. Zaddy was like Barack Obama, just came out of nowhere and I wish he would have stayed wherever he was at. I remember we had crossed paths while I was out driving around town on a beautiful day. He was driving a nice car and I was in a hooptie when he flagged me down. Zaddy kept a nice luxurious car. Bait, at the time, for silly young females like myself at the time. He invited me to check out a new hang out spot in the area. He wasn't inviting me out on a date but making me aware of the new club in town, in case I wanted to check it out. My hometown is small and there are not a lot of attractions. There are annual basketball tournaments, black expos, and social gatherings scattered throughout the year and that is about it. You literally have to be creative to make Muncie fun and exciting.

> A wolf dressed in sheep's clothing.

I wasn't a party girl since I had 4 young sons and no reliable babysitter, at the time. I hung out from time to time but I was mainly a homebody. I decided to check out the new local spot one evening and sure enough, Zaddy was there eyeing me down like a hawk lol. I locked eyes with him and "smooth operator" gradually made his way to my table. He was so handsome, sheepish, and kind; a wolf dressed in sheep's clothing to be quite frank.

Zaddy led me to believe he was single and available but I ended up becoming a side chick, by default, due to his deception. He initially told me his estranged girlfriend and child were living with him temporarily as they were supposed to be transitioning to another city. I thought the arrangement with the estranged girlfriend was odd but I brushed it off because it sounded good to someone that was young and enamored with this older man and his good looks.

I should have known better because he never disclosed where he lived nor extended an invitation for me to come over and chill. He was sneaky. We could only talk and see each other on his terms. But he called me daily, whispered sweet NOTHINGS in my ear and would come see me during booty call hours, so I was content for a little while. I thought eventually she would relocate and then he and I could be together. I had already envisioned my wedding dress, the ring, and chapel. Boy, was I living in La La land because I was in for a rude awakening

Zaddy not only had an estranged girlfriend living with him but multiple women. His array of women couldn't wait to brag about being his new love interest. News travels faster than Usain Bolt, in a small town, so it wouldn't take long for me to find out! His actions supported the rumors. Calls and late-night visits had dwindled, so I knew he was spreading himself thin like butter in an attempt to juggle all his women.

I didn't waste any time confronting him. I may have been young and naïve but I was a good detective. After my interrogation, he admitted that he was in a relationship with his child's mother but never with the other women. I should have run like Forrest, at this point. I knew he wasn't telling the truth. I guess I was supposed to believe that I was the only side chick. He lied about having a girlfriend in the first place, so no telling what else he would lie about. I remained one of his side chicks and demanded more of his time. It didn't work. Zaddy did what he wanted to do.

Girlfriend, if a man is willing to cheat on his wife and/or girlfriend to be with you, don't believe that he will be faithful to you. Trust me, he has others in rotation. I accepted the modern-day concubine role like a dummy since I had willingly given him my heart, mind, and body. A piece of man was better than no man, right? No ma'am! It cost me my peace of mind!

To make a long story short, I decided to get off of the emotional roller coaster ride after several months, that seemed like eternity. Zaddy didn't love me and I knew he never would. It was a hard pill to swallow. "Players only love you when they're playing." Like Keyshia Cole said, "I had had enough of no love" so she (live in girlfriend) and the rest of his women could have him. I was tired of being his plaything. The sad part is, I tolerated all this nonsense and the only things I had to show for it was a cheap necklace made out of tin and a knock off purse that I swear he hijacked from his girlfriend's closet.

The late and great poetess, Maya Angelou said, "when a person shows you who they are, believe them". We need to

> "When a person shows you who they are, believe them"

apply this principle to all of our relationships. Actions speak louder than words. If what a person says and what they do are in conflict with one another, consistently, they are revealing their true character and aren't trustworthy.

Sometimes we can't see the forest for the trees. Ask God to show you what the devil doesn't want you to see. We can get so blinded by how a man looks and what he has, that we miss the red flags. Satan is gorgeous! He disguises himself as the Angel of Light. Imposters can resemble the real thing. God has answered that simple prayer every time and He will do the same for you.

And don't beat yourself up if you intentionally ignored a red flag. Learn the lessons, guard your heart, and trust your instincts. God is merciful and gracious. He restores our soul, binds up our wounds, and mends our broken hearts.

**Reflect on a time you ignored a red flag (s)? Can you identify the red flag (s)? Did the relationship end due to the red flag you ignored from the beginning?**

_____

_____

_____

_____

_____

_____

_____

_____

_____

# Don't Settle

———∞·∞———

*Don't settle for less than God's best*

*"What you want exists. Don't settle until you get it.*
*#Inspiration*

Have you ever desired a Chanel purse, Gucci belt, or Louis Vuitton luggage but couldn't afford it, so you settled for the knock off brand instead? Some of us will even settle for the knock off just to have that logo broadcasted on the purse we carry on our shoulder or the shoes we wear on our feet. "Fake it to make it", I guess or trying to keep up with the Joneses. We tend to choose our man like this. We will settle for the knock off, for a number or reasons, instead of waiting for the real one to show up.

Perhaps we are impatient or think we won't ever meet the man of our dreams, so we just

> We just settle to say we 'got a man'.

settle to say we 'got a man' because we fear being alone, don't like being alone, or because everyone around us is 'booed' up. Maybe you don't know your worth and settle for a lowlife just to fulfill your desire to be married. Whatever the reason, settling has dire consequences and can lead to unhappiness in so many areas of your life. My own experience led to verbal, emotional, and physical abuse.

I remember being in pain, lonely, and vulnerable after I ended things with Zaddy. I was raising sons by myself. Cooking, cleaning, driving to basketball and football practices and games, trying to assist with homework and do my own, because I was in school just like the kids. I was parenting, working, and attending church when I could. Whew child, I'm getting exhausted just going down memory lane! God obviously had His hands on me!!

Your girl just wanted comfort and help. And we all know one way to get over one man is to get under another one, correct? Hail naw!! That is a lie from the pits of Hell! You are just pacifying the pain and possibly jumping out of one frying pan into another. You more than likely are too hurt, unstable, and broken to make rational decisions and end up compounding pain on top of pain when you learn the new man is a carbon copy of the last one or worse, in my case. When you don't take time to heal and ponder on your errors with the last man or identify the lesson (s) you learned from the last relationship, you end up carrying baggage from one relationship to another like a "bag lady" (where my Erykah Badu fans).

So, the first cute guy that took interest in me, was actually single, and didn't mind me having four kids by four different men, was like a savior! I didn't think I could find a man that would truly love me and my kids, so when Tyrone didn't seem to mind, I thought he was the one. An answer to a prayer so I thought.

Tyrone had lucked up and found a young woman that was in pain, had no standards, didn't know her worth, and desired to be married. All of it worked to his advantage for a little while. He was fresh out of the penitentiary, which made him fresh meat to the single ladies. I basically met this man on a Tuesday, we were boyfriend and girlfriend by Wednesday, and living with one another by Friday. This is a little fictitious but the point I'm getting at is we didn't know each other and were moving way too fast.

I didn't know this man from Adam and moved him in with me and my kids. I don't recall knowing why Tyrone got locked up initially but for all I knew he could have been a murderer, rapist, or pedophile. I was putting myself and children in danger because I had to have a man. Yeah, I was one of those women during that chapter in my life. He seemed nice, was tall, dark, well-kept, and accepted my kids, so I just carried on like a foolish dame.

Well, my foolery got me choked out multiple times, loaded 9 mm guns lodged to my head, beat with one hand while he was driving and the other hand on steering wheel, dragged off of porches, abused in front of relatives, and suffered many blows to my head while I was in a relationship with him. To this day I wonder if that abuse has caused issues with my memory? Or is it just called being middle aged? Lol!

Tyrone had a lot of rage I didn't know about. He resorted to violence to settle verbal altercations. I know I had a smart mouth but I didn't deserve to be hit with a closed fist because of it. I think most of our arguments generated from me finding out he was cheating on me. I would confront him and the only way to shut me up was to get physical with me. He would apologize afterwards and make up for hitting me with epic sex.

I finally mustered up the strength to break up with him, not only for my sake but my kid's sake. I knew they would not be little boys forever and would one day attempt to hurt Tyrone for harming their mother. Then they would possibly be in trouble with the law because of my ignorance. But I would still mess around with Tyrone every now and then because he was a good lover. You know how that goes. However, he still had the audacity to put his hands on me from time to time.

I can remember hanging out at a local night club and Tyrone spat in my face, picked me up, and bear hugged me because I was standing next to a guy I had previously dated. He had a whole girlfriend that he was living with and still assaulting me. On another occasion, I remember him pouring beer on me at a club when I was on the dance floor shaking it like a tail feather with a gentleman. Tyrone was out with his girlfriend, at the time, but was all up in my business. He didn't want me but didn't want me to be with anyone else, I assume.

Thank God I finally decided to make Jesus my Lord and Savior and not just another church goer. Jesus set me free and helped me close the door to that abusive relationship and I never reopened it. "It ain't worth it Mizz Celie." No sex is good enough to be beat like meat being tenderized with a mallet.

What had taken some women years, disfigurement, dismemberment, and/or death to escape the torture of domestic violence, God rescued me in less than a year. When I hear about women suffering burns from acid on their faces, brokens limbs, or horrific deaths, I think how that could have been me, it should have been me, if it wasn't for the blood...in my Clark Sister's voice!

> Wait for God's best for you.

I'm thankful Tyrone never hurt my children. Some children aren't as fortunate. Too often children are molested, physically abused, and even killed by their mother's boyfriends. Our poor choices don't just affect us but can have damaging lifelong effects to our children and those closest to us. Please don't allow loneliness, desperation, and impatience cause you to settle and put yourself and others around you in danger.

Settling is a setback, and an adversary to happiness and fulfillment. It's a road to regret. Be patient, don't compromise, and wait for God's best for you.

**Have you ever settled? If so, what caused you to settle? What was the outcome?**

_____

_____

_____

_____

_____

_____

_____

_____

_____

_____

# TIP # 3

# Avoid The Messiah Complex

—⬦—

*Be still and know you are not God*

**– Quantia**

Problem-solving is one of my greatest strengths. Fixing things that are broken. I like a challenge. You got a problem; I got a solution. If I don't have a solution, I'm going to find one. It's like an adrenaline rush! I had to learn the hard way that it can be one of my greatest weaknesses also. Solving problems turned into me trying to fix people. I tried fixing an ex-felon and failed miserably. It only revealed how I needed Jesus to fix me!

> I needed Jesus to fix me!

Let me tell you about Jake. He was what we black folks call "light-skinned" or "high-yellow". He wasn't the most attractive man I had ever entertained. Jake was rough around the edges and possessed a bad boy nature that I had grown accustomed to. He had just served a long bid and was out on parole. Jake was straight hood! Chile, I thought nothing was wrong with a little thug passion.

I just knew I could save him before the streets got ahold of him again. I didn't want him to recidivate and return to prison, like approximately 70% of released offenders. I could even lead him to Christ. I would take him to church on Sundays so he could eventually accept Christ as His Lord and Savior. I was ready to perform an extreme makeover on this man with potential. Hahaha! I was the one that ended up with the extreme makeover. Hair fell out, skin aged, and I lost weight. He never became a Christian and I became a bad witness for Christ. Trust me, I retired from the construction industry after this wreckage.

At any rate, Jake started off with the love bombs the first time he reached out to me on one of my social media accounts. He wasn't a complete stranger. We had crossed paths a couple of times before he was incarcerated. He would blow up my phone and drop tons of compliments. Jake appeared to be down to earth, fun, and spontaneous. He balanced out my rather reserved and routine lifestyle so I thought we complimented each other well. We could talk for hours about anything. He even started attending church with me. My conversion plan was working! Syke! Master manipulators will do practically anything to get what they want from a person.

Jake shared his humble beginnings with me and didn't have the greatest childhood. I thought we were growing closer, since he was opening up to me. Family and friends had abandoned him at some point in his life. He told me one day if it wasn't for bad luck, he wouldn't have no luck at all. I felt so bad for him and desired to debunk that myth. I wanted to rescue him from the past trauma and pain that he shared with me. He knew how to pull at my heartstrings. Manipulation at its finest.

I discovered, early on, that Jake had been pursuing a whole other woman at the same time! I stumbled across this piece of information when I saw her picture on his screensaver. I knew it wasn't his mother or sister and it definitely wasn't me. He had me thinking I was his soulmate. I confronted him and he denied having any type of romantic relationship with her. I knew better than to date a man that had been recently released from prison. I had dated ex-felons before and got burnt every time but I thought this time would be different. He had me convinced that I was his soulmate.

Jake finally confessed that she was someone from his past and he had feelings for her. He said that he had feelings for me as well, and begged me to give him time to choose between the two of us. I did, against my better judgment. I allowed him to put me in a twisted version of "the boy is mine'. If you're my age you should remember that collaboration between Brandy and Monica. Thank goodness it never got that far. I'm not the confrontational type and I'm sure she didn't know about me.

If she did, I probably was painted as some crazy person that wouldn't let go. Besides he wasn't technically my man so I had no leverage.

Jake had built me up, only to tear me down. He began criticizing me. My hair was too nappy for him, all of a sudden. It wasn't an issue when he was dropping love bombs in the beginning. I didn't have 3A hair, like "Becky with the good hair", on his screensaver. If you're a natural sistah, you know what that means haha! He would compare my body to a certain actress. Hinting that "she" was in good shape at her age. He was running my self-esteem through the mill.

> He was gaining but I was losing.

I was behaving like a re-entry case manager. Assisting him with job applications, writing up resumes, teaching him how to use social media properly and tips to avoid being scammed while on different platforms. I even though about launching a nonprofit to help ex-felons get reacclimated to society. At least I could get grants and finances for my efforts. I wasn't getting anything for helping him, only misused and the blues. He was gaining but I was losing. Whatever he needed, I was providing. He was taking but not giving.

I started losing myself in this man, as you can see. I didn't know who I was anymore. I was in a state of rebellion. I was spending less time with God and focusing on Jake more. The Bible says, bad company corrupts good morals (1st Corinthians 15:33). He wasn't drawing me closer to God. In fact, he was feeding my flesh and not my soul. I was practicing celibacy but trying to please him, I compromised.

I found myself in competition with the other woman. I desired to show him I was every woman, like Chaka khan, and he didn't need her. He had awakened my love (lust) and I wasn't giving up that easy. Words to the wise, when another woman has a man's heart, there ain't nothing you can do about it. He may be with you physically but he is mentally and emotionally attached to her. My intuition told me he was going to choose her but I still had hope.

Jake invited me to chill with him one day after work. He had recently transitioned to another state and I drove over 100 miles overnight to be with him. We talked about exploring this new city together during my weekend visit. I made a hotel reservation before I left, since he was staying with relatives and didn't have his own place. I picked him up when I arrived since he didn't have his own means of transportation. We Netflix, chilled and fell asleep early, since he had to be at work before dusk. While driving him to work, he was very quiet when he exited the car, he wouldn't look at me. Odd. He said he would call later and shut the door.

I headed back to the hotel, looking forward to painting the town red, once he got off of work. Well, I received a text from him not too long after I dropped him. Jake informed me that he and Becky were taking their relationship to another level and he couldn't see me anymore. I felt so rejected, humiliated, and abandoned.

Here I was, in an unfamiliar city, hours away from home and alone in a hotel room that was paid for until the next day. I was so hurt. I could blame no one but myself. I had to repent to God for what I had done. He warned me about this man. Showed me all the signs but I thought I could change him. The late Ravi Zacharias said, "sin will take you farther than you want to go, keep you longer than you want to stay and cost you more than you want to pay."

I will let God be God.

At the end of the day, this brotha turned out to be way above my pay grade. The valuable lesson I learned is, you can't change or fix anyone. They have to want to change. You can barely fix yourself, let alone someone else. You will end up changing who you are, trying to change someone else. I will let God be God and stay in my lane. No more missionary dating for me.

Caution...If you are dating someone that has been released from prison recently, please have them tested from A to Z for any disease. You don't know what these men might be carrying in their bloodstream. They get tattoos with homemade needles which can expose them to hepatitis and some live double lives that can expose them to HIV/AIDS. I know firsthand because I worked at a male prison before. Protect yourself not only spiritually and emotionally but physically as well.

**Do you suffer from the Savior Complex? Do you attempt to fix others? Have you been successful?**

_____

_____

_____

_____

_____

_____

_____

_____

_____

_____

_____

# TIP # 4

# Establish Boundaries

———∞·∞———

*"'The only people who get upset about you setting boundaries, are those who were benefiting from you having none"*

**– Unknown**

Dr. Henry Cloud and Dr. John Townsend explains boundaries in a simple analogy in their best-selling book, Boundaries:

> What is our responsibility and what isn't.

"Just as homeowners set physical property lines around their land, we need to set mental, physical, emotional, and spiritual boundaries for our lives to help us distinguish what is our responsibility and what isn't." (Boundaries pg.28)

Boundaries are abstract borders that you put in place to protect your overall well-being. You need to establish healthy boundaries with family members, mentors, pastors, co-workers, friends and others. Individuals closest to you can overstep your boundaries intentionally or unintentionally, especially when they find out you have the disease to please. They will try to make their problems, issues, and responsibilities your problems, issues, and responsibilities. It's nothing wrong with helping if you can but please don't enable and help people take your kindness as a weakness. It's actually one of your best attributes.

Prime example, girlfriends are guilty of providing wife benefits without commitment. We do laundry, cook meals, clean, and give up our prized possession without bearing his last name. Judge Lynn Toler says, "never perform wife duties at girlfriend prices". "Why buy the cow when you can get the milk for free"? Beyonce told you if he like it then he needs to put a ring on it. Stay in your lane, honey.

You have to know where to draw the line in the sand and establish healthy boundaries

> Be upfront and clear about your expectations.

with those you love and may possibly fall in love with. Be upfront and clear about your expectations. Then you will know if someone is not respecting them. Don't widen your boundaries just to please people either. You give them an inch; they will take it a mile. If they are crossing your boundaries, you need to politely reinforce what you can and won't do. If they care about you, they will listen and respect your boundaries. If they don't listen, you might have to severe the relationship and gain control of your life again.

I love helping others but it can get me in trouble sometimes. I learned the hard way that people will only do what you allow them to do to you. Your lover, friend, child, etc. They will begin to take advantage of you and take you for granted. And people tend to lose respect for anyone they can run over. They won't take you seriously and end up just trying to get what they can get from you.

I can remember befriending older Christian women because they were wise, nurturing, and kind to me. These women were like big sisters and surrogate mothers. They would begin asking me for favors and I didn't mind. One would borrow money. They were my elders and if I could help in any way, I would. Well, it got to a point where they would only reach out to me when they wanted me to do something for them. I would get anxiety when I saw their phone numbers flash across my cell phone screen. I knew they just wanted a "favor".

I couldn't blame them because I allowed them to inconvenience me constantly and had conditioned them to only contact me when they needed something or wanted something done. They were like Pavlov's dogs! (Google this study if you're not familiar with it) Honestly, some things they could do themselves but why when Quantia could just do it?

These types of relationships began to take a toll on me spiritually, mentally, emotionally and physically. You can get so caught up in helping others fulfill their goals, visions, and dreams that you lose sight of your own. I had to set stricter boundaries and focus on my life again. When I stopped overextending myself, I didn't hear from some of them again.

> Learn to just say "no".

Learn to just say "no". You will feel like a new person and liberated. There are nicer ways to say it if it's still difficult to utter that small yet powerful word. However you choose to communicate it, see how many people will stick around. Or think of a time you told someone "no" or that you couldn't assist them. Did they continue to contact you? Saying "no" and establishing boundaries will separate the real from the fake. You will discover those who are truly a part of your tribe and those that were only around because of the gifts and talents you possessed, and what you could do for them.

I have another cautionary tale that involves a man I worked with years ago. We will call him Mr. Congeniality. Trust me the name suits him. He was so friendly and outgoing. Everyone adored him.

Mr. Congeniality was nerdish and hoodish all at the same time. He had charisma and good looks to add to his resume. He had a gift to gab and probably could charm the pants off of any woman. Mr. Congeniality was ambitious and a bag chaser. He was not committed to any position four too long and would divorce an employer that wasn't willing to pay him what he thought he was worth, in a heartbeat. He knew his value and would chuck up the deuces and be on to the next one in a split second.

I admired him from afar. By any means necessary, he would do anything to take care of his family and get a piece, or should I say the whole, American pie. He was a natural leader and would motivate me to chase after my own dreams and not sell myself short. Mr. Congeniality was like my life coach. I was dating a friend of his at the time. He tried to warn me about the man with subtle hints. He didn't want to be blunt and risk their friendship. I appreciated the warning and eventually broke it off with the dude because he was certified crazy.

Mr. Congeniality was so easy to talk to and I could be myself around him. I knew he was off limits because he was married with children. Since we worked together, we saw nothing wrong with exchanging phone numbers. He would call from time to time to check up on me. Request prayers and advice. I had started becoming attracted to him and I knew he was feeling the same way. The Holy Spirit was convicting me and urging me to end our "friendly" contacts.

We were on a slippery slope at this point. But we continued to reach out to each other, and more frequently. I had even met up with him at local establishments a couple of times. I justified it because it was supposed to be business related. In all actuality, we could have e-mailed each other to discuss business acumen. Again, I was convicted. I had to put myself in his wife's shoes and ask myself would I be okay with my husband meeting up with a single woman I don't know anything about nor never met?

What started off as just a normal workplace relationship started evolving into an emotional affair. I knew I had to put the brakes on it. Our conversations started becoming too personal and nothing was off limits. He started mentioning his needs needed to be met because wifey couldn't fulfill all of them. He even admitted to having different affairs throughout his marriage. I don't know if he had an ulterior motive all along but I knew that was a cue to exit stage left.

I was no longer a modern-day concubine and knew the emptiness, loneliness,

> You can't play with fire and not expect to get burnt.

condemnation, shame and guilt I felt when I was a mistress. I had to remind Mr. Congeniality and myself that he had commitments and obligations that couldn't be breached and I wasn't a 2nd class citizen. I knew my value and worth at this point in my life. Therefore, this once friendly workplace relationship had to end. You can't play with fire and not expect to get burnt.

This wasn't my first rodeo with a married man and I should have set strict boundaries from the beginning. I wasn't his wife and therefore should not have been his confidante. It seemed so innocent but Satan uses the same ole tricks to trip us up. He just dresses them up in a different package. He is always out to kill, steal, and destroy. Destroy marriages, kill friendships, and steal your joy. God had delivered me from the sin of adultery and I was determined to stay free.

Please set healthy boundaries both for your sake and others. They will help you save or salvage some relationships and determine which ones need to be severed. You will avoid being burned out mentally, emotionally, spiritually, and physically while others are living their best life at your expense. Teach people how to treat you and channel your energy to individuals that respect you and your boundaries.

**Are you a people pleaser and tend to overextend yourself? If so, how? What boundaries will you begin to establish first?**

_____

_____

_____

_____

_____

_____

_____

_____

_____

_____

_____

_____

_____

# TIP # 5

# Raise Your Standards

––––––∞·∞––––––

*"Keep you heels, head, and standards high"*

## – Coco Chanel

According to Google, a "standard" is a level of quality or attainment. Do you remember in school athletes were held at a higher standard than their peers? They couldn't have behavioral issues because they represented their school in spirit and deed. Have you heard someone say I prefer quality over quantity? Essentially, what they are saying is that they prefer something that is solid and will last a long-time vs cheap and only last a short-term. I prefer organic over non-organic because it's supposed to be better for you. It has stricter regulations and less pesticides than non-organic food. Same with men. Some come with more pesticides and poison than others. It all depends on the caliber of the man.

There was this guy I had known for a while; I will call him Thirsty. Initially, I had a lot respect for him because I saw how God transformed his life and allowed him to overcome many obstacles. From my recollection, in the beginning, he was a humble Christian. However, I watched his ego go from 0 to 7 on the Richter scale over the years and I refused to be one of his victims. We never dated but he would try to shoot his shot every chance he got! He bricked every time. I was just unchartered territory and he was like a dog chasing the cat!

> He was a successful man on paper.

Thirsty was used to throwing his weight around. He was a successful man on paper. A lot of women were enamored by his swag. He was a charmer, educated, and dapper. He could dress his butt off! Be cleaner than the board of health! Thirsty would prey, not pray, on single Christian women that desired to be married, from my observation. To be honest, no woman was exempt. She could be a heathen, your sister, cousin, or friend! Thirsty needed deliverance from lust and fornication, in my opinion.

I knew someone that really adored him and was so excited when he approached her. She thought she had found her Boaz. More like Bozo the clown. Of course, she made the error of sleeping with him after only a couple of phone calls. He disappeared after a few late-night creeps. I felt so bad for her because she thought she had a chance. You could tell this was his "M.O." Thirsty didn't know she had told me about their secret rendezvous. I was the next one on his hit list. Remember, he hadn't conquered me so I was a challenge.

After he pestered me for a while and acted like I was just his homie, I finally agreed to meet up with him for dinner one day. To my defense, we did call each other homies. I was trying to inform him that he was in the friend zone. That didn't stop him from trying to knock my boots. Again, he had a big ego. I guess he was trying to make me his "homey, lover, friend" but I don't think so homey the clown. Meanwhile, he talked about himself the whole darn time. Every other sentence began with "I" and who wanted him. Thirsty appeared self-absorbed and narcissistic-ish to me.

After dinner, he had the audacity to invite me to a hotel room not once but twice. I was dumbfounded and shut him down with the quickness! I try to tell women; these kinds of men be expecting "the honey after they spend their money'. Of course, all men aren't this grimy. If you use the blues clues (red flags) mentioned in the previous chapters, you will know which ones are genuine and which ones are thirsty, like Thirsty. Even Christian men, obviously. Even after this encounter, Thirsty tried to pursue me years later.

I always believe people can change because God has changed me but I was willing

> God is no respecter of persons.

to participate in the transformation also. God is no respecter of persons, so what He has done for me, He can do for others.

Deliverance, freedom, and healing isn't just for me but everybody that desires to be liberated from sin and bondage. Sometimes this mindset can get me in trouble though. I said all that to say, I tried to give Thirsty another chance to redeem himself and prove he could be just my brother in Christ, since a few years had passed since our first dinner date. Chile, he was worse!

I recall him reaching out again after I liked a post on one of his social media accounts. He called me then started a series of text messages. Thirsty consistently tried to get me to come to his house. There was no longer an invitation for dinner. He went straight for the gusto! I assume he wasn't spending any more money on me since I didn't give up the nookie/yoni after the dinner he purchased years prior. This time I assume he would take the cheap approach and would have nothing to lose if I didn't sleep with him. He fits the description of a typical womanizer.

One weekend night he texted me stating he was laying in his king size bed all alone and desired some company. My mind flashbacked to Alexander O'Neal crooning, 'this bed is too big for me to be in all alone". This is grown folk's music haha! Thirsty was still going to be in his bed alone because I was not falling for that old booty call trick. This man was bold and wanted what he wanted which was obviously some Quantia, lol! He bypassed dinner and went straight for dessert!

I figured this "just come over and chill" tactic had worked for him with silly women. I won't judge because I used to be a silly and desperate woman. It probably worked 99% of the time so he felt the odds were in his favor. I learned men will recycle the same ridiculous pickup lines to practically every woman that crosses their path. Shoot if it isn't broke, don't fix it. Some women probably assumed because he is a Christian, his motives were pure. The devil is a lie!

I had politely checked Thirsty for his unflavored advance. He had a lame rebuttal of course, like the last time. This dude was slick as oil. Each time he would try to seduce me, he would attempt to save face and say he was just bored and wanted company to watch a movie with. Who goes to a hotel or comes to his house just to watch a movie late at night? I guess I had "fool" branded on my forehead or something. You could have watched a movie if you were so bored. Or how about go to sleep? He attempted to play on my intelligence. Now he needed deliverance from lying! Thirsty wasn't fooling nobody but himself. After this incident, I ghosted him since my words meant nothing to him. I wouldn't waste my breath trying to help this man get a clue. It was like talking to a brick wall. I ignored his calls and texts and he eventually quit reaching out to me. I gave him a chance to redeem himself and he blew it.

> Don't fall for the okie doke.

Moral of the story ladies, don't fall for the okie doke. All Christian men aren't equal and you don't want to be unequally yoked with a man like Thirsty. Men like this look good on paper. He had money, status, nice clothes, cars, etc. He knew the Word but so does the devil. I was not impressed by what he had accumulated materially. His pride outweighed what he had. He was superficial and had no substance, from what I gathered. I had to raise my standards to avoid men like him in the future and I would advise you to do the same. When the enemy comes in like a flood, God will raise the standard (Isaiah 59:19).

You will be surprised how many women haven't really thought about what their

> Make a list of specific standards.

standards are. If you have no, to low standards or don't know what they are, it's like going to the grocery store without a grocery list. You don't know what you want and end up buying what you don't need or something unhealthy. I had a general idea about what I desired in a man but I had to be very specific after my encounter with him. I definitely prefer character over coins, thanks to this experience. It's time to make a list of specific standards and don't renege on them. You can change them as you evolve but make sure the quality remains.

**What are your standards? Are your standards to low or high? Do you believe that what you want, exist?**

_____

_____

_____

_____

_____

_____

_____

_____

_____

_____

_____

_____

_____

_____

# TIP # 6

# Build Your Relationship With God

———∞·∞———

*"Jesus is the best thing that ever happened to me"*

**– Martha Munizzi**

The most important relationship you will ever have is with God. He desires an intimate and personal relationship with us, and we should desire the same type of relationship with Him. Jesus revealed the Great Commandment to us in Matthew 22:37, "Love the Lord with all your heart, with all your soul, and with all your mind."

We are to love Him with everything we got! Our minds, | He desires all of you.

our hearts, our souls and our bodies should love and reverence God. We have a tendency to pick and choose which part of us we will honor God with. Some of us may love Him with our mind but not honor Him with our bodies. He desires your body. Apostle Paul reminds us in Romans 12:1, "present your bodies a living sacrifice, holy, acceptable to God, *which is* your reasonable service." He desires all of you and not bits and pieces.

God gives us access to all of Him so, why should we hold anything back from our Creator? Thank goodness He understands our human frailty and is patient with us. God knows we aren't perfect. He knows transformation is a process. However, we should be striving towards perfection and not use the excuse, nobody's perfect, to live ungodly.

Why should I get to know God and establish a relationship with Him? I can give you a few reasons. For starters He created the Heavens and the Earth. You and me. Our family and friends. He is all knowing, meaning He knows everything! A gazillion things! He has more power than all the rulers on this Earth put together. He has way more power than the devil. You have to remember God created the devil. Whom, at one time, was the most beautiful angel. That's why he can disguise himself as the angel of light and creep into your life as a good man or friend. God is omnipresent which means He is everywhere. You can't run or hide from Him. King David said if he made his bed in Hell, God would be there (Psalm 139:8). No human can do what God can do.

I don't know about you but I want someone like God on my team. I would want to know more about this powerhouse. I can ask Him anything and He won't judge me. He has a solution to all my problems. Keeps my secrets. He doesn't gossip and backbite. Sounds like one heck of a trustworthy friend. He won't cheat on you. Lie to you. Abuse and abandon you. Manipulate you. He will treat you better than a spouse, parent, or friend. God always has your back and isn't fickle like us human beings. All these reasons are enough to win me over! And it's not even a fraction of who He is or what He is capable of doing. I don't know about you but I'm souled out!!

How do I get to know God or know Him better and build a relationship with Him? I'm glad you asked. Think about how you get to know anyone that sparks your interest. You desire communication and quality time with them. You call them regularly because you want to hear their voice or you make plans to see them so you can bask in their positive energy. When you do talk or see each other, you ask 21 questions because you desire to know more about them. You get to know them instead of relying on what people say about them. We know people can be biased, so you have to form your own opinion.

> Spend time in His Word, the Bible.

It's no different with getting to know God. You spend time in His Word, the Bible. Some say it's "Basic Instructions Before Leaving Earth" and I would concur. It's one way, and probably the most effective way, to learn about His nature and character. You communicate with God through prayer which is basically talking to Him. He doesn't mind you asking Him complex questions such as, why you can't find a good man. Trust me, He can't wait to fill you in. You have to be open to His questions also. Remember a relationship with God isn't one-sided just because you can't see Him in physical form. You expect things from Him and He has expectations of you as well.

Jesus teaches us in John 14:21, "He who has My

His grace is sufficient.

commandments and keeps them, it is he who loves Me." The "he" in that scripture refers to you and I, and anyone that professes to be a child of God. God expects you to obey Him and follow His instructions. Again, He knows we will fall short of His glory and His grace is sufficient. But remember, His grace isn't a license to sin. It's there just in case, like auto insurance.

In fact, the book of Jude says, God can keep us from falling. We don't always have to fall down and bump our heads. If we will listen and obey God, we can avoid unhealthy relationships like the ones I shared with you in this book. God always gives us wisdom and even warnings about the people that cross our paths. Even if we get caught up in a toxic relationship because we were disobedient, impatient, or hard-headed, He will make a way of escape for us. We just have to be willing to exit and run like Forrest!

God's will for your life is perfect, good, and pleasing, according to Romans 12:2. He knows the plans He has for you; they will prosper and not harm you. You first have to seek Him to know what is good, perfect, and pleasing. Then you won't be living like a broken compass with no direction and end up at the wrong place or even lost.

Some of us are living outside of His perfect will for our lives because we have failed to include Him in the details of our lives. Surviving instead of thriving. Existing rather than living. The lyricist Drake said it best..." everyone dies but not everyone lives." I don't know about you but I want to live the abundant life Jesus promised.

When you keep God first and obey His instructions, you will experience all the good things He has in store for you. Matthew 6:33 instructs us to "seek ye first the kingdom of God and His righteousness and all these things shall be added". His wisdom, peace, joy, favor, desire of your heart, fruitful relationships and so much more!

**Do you want to know God better? What steps will you take to build your relationship with God? When will you begin?**

_____

_____

_____

_____

_____

_____

_____

_____

_____

_____

_____

_____

_____

_____

# Become Your Own Best Friend

—∽·∾—

*Love yourself*

*"Loving yourself isn't vanity, it's sanity"*

**– Unknown**

What is love? Webster's definition is an intense feeling of deep affection for

God is the Epitome of Love

someone and a pleasure or interest in something. God is the epitome of love and Jesus' death on cross is the best example of how it is expressed. "God so loved the world that He gave His only begotten Son so that everyone who believes in Him, shall not perish but have everlasting life" (John 3:16). Jesus loved us so much that He died a gruesome death for sins He didn't commit so we could live. Now that's love!! God set the bar high!

The Bible says in 1 Corinthians 13:4, "love is patient, kind, love is not jealous, or boastful or proud or rude, longs suffering" and many other positive qualities. This means love is not

48

impatient, unkind, abusive, mean, jealous, proud, superficial or manipulative. I began to apply what God taught me in His word and started loving myself from the inside out. Unconditionally and properly.

I love me because God first loved me (1 John 4:19) and Jesus commands self-love in Matthew 22:36. It is the 2nd part of the Great Commandment. Love your neighbor like you love yourself. I can only truly love my neighbor if I sincerely love myself. I also know He made me in His image and likeness and put His stamp of approval on me. That let me know I have value and worth. More reasons to love myself!

Loving yourself is not always easy, by no means. I have flaws and imperfections that I need to improve and/or embrace. I wake up not on fleek most days! I gently remind myself beauty is skin deep. It's what's beneath the surface that truly matters because what's on the inside will radiate and manifest itself on the outside. I'm sure you know a woman that is gorgeous on the outside but has a nasty attitude. The bad attitude can sometimes paint over the beautiful exterior and cause her to appear unattractive. I put more stock in my character than Clinique. Looks fade but a woman who fears the Lord is to be praised (Proverbs 31:30).

When was the last time you told yourself, I love you? Have you ever told yourself that you love you? Don't worry, I'm guilty.

It's been a while since I said those 3 words to myself. But I make sure I express it through my actions towards myself. Matter a fact, let's pause for the cause right now and tell ourselves how much we love and appreciate ourselves. Follow my lead. Quantia, girl I love me some you! Awkward? Sounds a little conceited or narcissistic, right? Wrong!! Remember Jesus has given us permission to love ourselves.

There is nothing prideful about loving yourself nor verbally affirming it. I'm

> Life and death are in the power of the tongue.

willing to bet some of us don't do it at all or nearly enough. It's so easy to tell your child, significant other, or parent that we love them. We may even verbally express it to our loved ones on a daily basis. But do we reiterate it to ourselves? We will tell ourselves how fat we are or how big our nose is. Call ourselves stupid and dumb. Life and death are in the power of the tongue and we will no longer speak curses but blessings over ourselves. It's time to tell ourselves how beautiful we are. How talented and creative we are. Give ourselves the grace and mercy we extend to others. Let's extend the olive branch to ourselves. Forgive ourselves. Make reconciliation with ourselves. Respect and honor ourselves. Do things that will make us better versions of ourselves.

After seeking God and Godly counsel, I decided to see a Christian Therapist to help me process and overcome the damaging effects of rejection, abandonment, and trauma I experienced growing up. These issues gave birth to low-esteem, promiscuity, and attachment issues. Trauma bonds and codependency are real. When left dormant, they can create havoc in your life and manifest itself in your relationships.

I know the black community frowns on therapy but I recommend it. The ones that protest it, probably really need it. With God, His Word, prayer, and the assistance of a therapist, I have experienced breakthrough after breakthrough, Glory to God! She encouraged me to have a healthy relationship with myself. I've been doing that ever since and encourage you to follow suit.

First starters, I took Beyonce's advice and became my own best friend. You should do the same. Have your own back. Stop handing out applications for someone to fulfill this role. You are the best candidate and applicant. No one can love you like you, except Jesus. You know you better than anyone else. Don't be afraid to hang out with yourself. You have to be comfortable with you, before others will. Treat yourself to a Sunday Brunch. Go to dinner and a movie. Travel alone if you have to. People do it all the time. Don't miss out on life because you supposedly have no one to explore it with. You got you!

| Being single isn't a disease. |
| :--- |

Contrary to popular belief, being single isn't a disease. Apostle Paul encouraged it (1 Corinthians 7:32-35). People equate singleness with loneliness, which is a lie from the pits of Hell. They often quote it's not good for man to be alone and immediately believe they need a "Bae". You can be in a marriage and be lonely, from my observation. Loneliness is a state of mind. You can be single and satisfied. Parents, children, and friends can be companions. Stay connected to God and the people He connects you with and you will be just fine.

Incorporate self-care in your daily regimen and life. Get adequate sleep which is about 7 to 8 hours per day. Exercise and be mindful of what you eat. What you eat could be killing you. My family knows that I am not a fan of, what I refer to as, slave food. I am no longer a slave and will not subject myself to chitlins, pig feet, and cow tongues! Gross! I'm not trying to offend anyone but these aren't the type of delicacies I want to splurge on. If you do like these detestable food items, I mean delectable food items, please enjoy them with moderation and at your own risk. Pamper yourself with a spa day. If you can't afford to go to one right now, bring the spa day to your home.

Play some jazz, light some candles, and decorate your bathtub with rose petals and your favorite essential oils. And as we talked about throughout this book, avoid or cut off toxic relationships.

Invest in yourself. Find your passion and pursue it. I bet if you put all that energy,

> Cultivate your gifts, talents, and skills.

time, money, and resources into yourself instead of a trifling man and people that misuse you, imagine what you can accomplish. You could be the CEO in your own company, write the next best seller, start your own non-profit, obtain a PhD, the possibilities are limitless. Invest in yourself. Learn what profession or trade compliments your character and capabilities. Go to school if you need a degree to obtain the position you desire. Cultivate your gifts, talents, and skills. Remember all things are possible with God on your side.

At the end of the day, when you have a relationship with God and love yourself, it will be difficult for others to mistreat, misuse, or abuse you. I encourage you to use the tips I suggested and develop your own relationship hacks so when you see crazies like Tyrone and Jake coming, you will cross the street!

# Phenomenally Me

———⊂✕·✕⊃———

I wanted to share with you one of my favorite poems by Maya Angelou. It showcases how confidence and love for yourself will separate you from all the others. You don't have to be the prettiest, the smartest, or the most talented woman in the room. Confidence in who you are, whose you are, and what you possess will make you attractive and appealing. It will allow the law of attraction to work in your favor. Attracting people that will add value to your life instead of subtracting from it.

> You are fearfully and wonderfully made!

You are fearfully and wonderfully made! God's masterpiece. A piece of divine art. Hand-crafted and custom-made. Folks have to buy what we are born with! No shade but facts. God doesn't make junk! God made you a woman for a reason. He made you on purpose and for a purpose. We are the carriers of life, nurturers, and the pillars of our families. Boss women, doctors, lawyers, mothers, teachers, and the list goes on. You are a phenomenal woman!

Pretty women wonder where my secret lies.
I'm not cute or built to suit a fashion model's size
But when I start to tell them,
They think I'm telling lies.
I say,
It's in the reach of my arms,
The span of my hips,
The stride of my step,
The curl of my lips.
I'm a woman
Phenomenally.
Phenomenal woman,
That's me.

I walk into a room
Just as cool as you please,
And to a man,
The fellows stand or
Fall down on their knees.
Then they swarm around me,
A hive of honey bees.
I say,
It's the fire in my eyes,
And the flash of my teeth,
The swing in my waist,
And the joy in my feet.
I'm a woman
Phenomenally.

Phenomenal woman,
That's me.

Men themselves have wondered
What they see in me.
They try so much
But they can't touch
My inner mystery.
When I try to show them,
They say they still can't see.
I say,
It's in the arch of my back,
The sun of my smile,
The ride of my breasts,
The grace of my style.
I'm a woman
Phenomenally.
Phenomenal woman,
That's me.

Now you understand
Just why my head's not bowed.
I don't shout or jump about
Or have to talk real loud.
When you see me passing,
It ought to make you proud.
I say,
It's in the click of my heels,
The bend of my hair,
the palm of my hand,
The need for my care.

’Cause I’m a woman
Phenomenally.
Phenomenal woman,
That’s me.

Maya Angelou

**Will you become your own best friend? Are verbal affirmations important to you? How will you incorporate self-care into your life?**

_____

_____

_____

_____

_____

_____

_____

_____

_____

_____

_____

_____

_____

Made in the USA
Coppell, TX
27 September 2021